Grief Therapy

August 2002

To my dear
sister, Irene!

I have one of these
for me! &I
think it's neat!

I love you.
Doris

Grief Therapy

written by
Karen Katafiasz

illustrated by
R.W. Alley

ONE
CARING
PLACE

Abbey Press

Text © 1993 by Karen Katafiasz
Illustrations © 1993 St. Meinrad Archabbey
Published by One Caring Place
Abbey Press
St. Meinrad, Indiana 47577

Library of Congress Catalog Number
93-72765

ISBN 0-87029-267-6

Printed in the United States of America

Foreword

Few events can affect your life as powerfully as the death of a loved one. Yet many people are uneasy speaking about death and dealing with the emotions that accompany it. The conventional wisdom tells survivors to "keep busy; don't dwell on your loss; just snap out of it." You may find yourself believing that. You may even doubt your own character strength and sanity when you haven't quickly returned to "normal."

But the conventional wisdom is wrong.

All the feelings that overwhelm you when a loved one dies deserve your attention. They are important openings to greater awareness: about the relationship you shared, your own needs, the meaning of life, the mystery of God's love. And they take time.

They are also the steps to your recovery, for there is no way *out* but *through.* Only by letting yourself experience grief can you move beyond it. *Beyond*—not to your old way of being or what once was "normal"; not to denial of your hurt; not to resentment and bitterness. But *beyond* to fully integrating loss into your life, to richer understanding, renewed purpose, deeper spirituality, rebirth.

Grieving is painful and demanding. But healing—profound, transforming healing—does come. *Grief Therapy* offers that promise and points the way.

1.

Respect the power of grief.
Know that it can affect you
psychologically, physically, and
spiritually in intense and
sometimes surprising ways.
Stay gentle with yourself.

2.

Be open to the pain of your broken heart. God enters through its brokenness.

3.

Remain open to the hurt. You may think it easier to suppress the pain or avoid it with distractions and busyness. But eventually your emotions will surface; grief will demand your attention.

FOOD

4.

Cry. Your tears testify to your love. And tears that spring from love help bring healing and renewal.

5.

Stay connected to others. You need their presence, their support, their concern, their listening, their hugs.

6.

Give yourself time to grieve. It may take several years just to accept the finality of a loss, that someone is gone forever, and even more to work through your emotions.

7.

The pattern of your grief is unique, shaped by your particular relationship, specific circumstances, and distinctive temperament. Ignore others' attempts to tell you how to feel or how long to feel.

8.

Expect to experience different stages in your grieving: shock, numbness, denial, depression, confusion, fear, anger, bitterness, guilt, regret, acceptance, hope. They may come in any order and any number of times.

9.

Forgive yourself: for being angry or disappointed with others, including the one who died and left you; for being powerless to have prevented the loss; for everything you wish you had or hadn't done.

10.

It's OK to be angry with God. Something seems unreal and terribly wrong now—something <u>is</u> wrong now—and you may feel cheated. Acknowledge that.

11.

Your loss is not God's punishment or God's attempt to test you. Know that God shares the hurt in your heart and wants to lead you to new hope and peace; know that God grieves with you.

12.

When some persons' attempts to comfort you only deepen the hurt, forgive them for not understanding. Later, when you comfort someone else, remember what not to say.

13.

Be with those who also are grieving. As you tell your stories, you will share an understanding of the heart that is deeper than words.

14.

Learn from those who have experienced healing after loss. Their survival is reassuring proof that you, too, will endure.

15.

Where your wound is, there can be your greatest contribution. You know what it is to be vulnerable and in pain. Let that knowledge open you to others who are hurting.

16.

In a letter, a poem, a drawing, a journal entry, or an imaginary conversation with the one you have lost, pour out the feelings you never had a chance to express. This will foster healing.

17.

Pray for and with the one who has died. The love between you is a spiritual bond that death cannot sever.

18.

Mourn not just for the loss of what was but also for what will never be. And then gently, lovingly let go.

19.

Undertake new activities and create new rituals out of the past. Through them you can maintain the memory of your loved one, even as you embark on a different chapter in your life.

20.

Make small beginnings toward reshaping your life without the one you loved. Your efforts are seeds of hope that you can cultivate into a fruitful new existence.

21.

Anniversaries and holidays—times that used to mean joy and celebration—can be among the toughest now. Observe them with care and simple ceremony to ease the pain.

22.

Celebrate your loved one with your own memories and the memories that others share with you. This celebration will keep your loved one with you and a part of you.

23.

Sometimes the best thing to do
is to comfort yourself with small
pleasures: a cup of tea, freshly
cut flowers, a soothing bath,
moments by the fire.

24.

In some ways, you never "get over" a significant loss. It inevitably changes you. You can choose whether that change is for the better.

25.

Sometimes your grief can be so overwhelming because it encompasses the grieving you never did for other, earlier losses in your life. Let yourself feel the pain of those losses too.

26.

When you find yourself doubting your capacity to recover, be patient and realize that the grief process, though lengthy, ultimately does bring healing.

27.

Let yourself feel good again, laugh with friends, have fun. Living your life to the full is not betrayal of a memory but fulfillment of a promise to someone who would want only the best for you.

28.

There may always be a small place within you that remains hollow. Value it. A quiet, abiding emptiness can be God's way of sustaining your connection to your loved one.

29.

When you feel that your loss has drained your life of all direction or meaning or joy, present your nothingness to God. God has never been closer.

30.

Life matters, no matter how long or short. And it lasts. Trust that God's promise of unending life is real and that your life today matters too.

31.

It may seem as if you'll never feel truly happy again. But be assured that you will—and your joy will have a richness and a depth that come from your having known profound pain and profound healing.

32.

Remind yourself of your reasons for living. You have a future worth enduring for, and you deserve to find a renewed sense of purpose and pleasure in your life.

33.

You will reach a point where you can finally go for an hour, or a day, or a week without painful reminders of absence and emptiness. Look for new awakenings. Be open to rebirth.

34.

You have learned that you are not always in control of life's circumstances. Use your new awareness to become more in rhythm with the flow of life, more in harmony with its song.

35.

Your grieving is among the most sacred and the most human things you will ever do. It will plummet you into the mystery of life…and death…and resurrection. Honor it.

Karen Katafiasz is a writer and editor whose books include *Finding Your Way Through Grief, Anger Therapy, Self-esteem Therapy, Christmas Therapy,* and *Celebrate-your-womanhood Therapy.* She lives in Santa Claus, Indiana, and works as assistant director of communications for the Sisters of St. Benedict of Ferdinand, Indiana.

Illustrator for the Abbey Press Elf-help Books, **R.W. Alley** also illustrates and writes children's books. He lives in Barrington, Rhode Island, with his wife, daughter, and son.

The Story of the Abbey Press Elves

The engaging figures that populate the Abbey Press "elf-help" line of publications and products first appeared in 1987 on the pages of a small self-help book called *Be-good-to-yourself Therapy*. Shaped by the publishing staff's vision and defined in R.W. Alley's inventive illustrations, they lived out author Cherry Hartman's gentle, self-nurturing advice with charm, poignancy, and humor.

Reader response was so enthusiastic that more Elf-help Books were soon under way, a still-growing series that has inspired a line of related gift products.

The especially endearing character featured in the early books—sporting a cap with a mood-changing candle in its peak—has since been joined by a spirited female elf with flowers in her hair.

These two exuberant, sensitive, resourceful, kindhearted, lovable sprites, along with their lively elfin community, reveal what's truly important as they offer messages of joy and wonder, playfulness and co-creation, wholeness and serenity, the miracle of life and the mystery of God's love.

With wisdom and whimsy, these little creatures with long noses demonstrate the elf-help way to a rich and fulfilling life.

Elf-help Books

...adding "a little character" and a lot of help to self-help reading!

Be-good-to-your-family Therapy
#20154 $4.95   ISBN 0-87029-300-1

Stress Therapy
#20153 $4.95   ISBN 0-87029-301-X

Making-sense-out-of-suffering Therapy
#20156 $4.95   ISBN 0-87029-296-X

Get Well Therapy
#20157 $4.95   ISBN 0-87029-297-8

Anger Therapy
#20127 $4.95   ISBN 0-87029-292-7

Caregiver Therapy
#20164 $4.95   ISBN 0-87029-285-4

Self-esteem Therapy
#20165 $4.95   ISBN 0-87029-280-3

Take-charge-of-your-life Therapy
#20168 $4.95   ISBN 0-87029-271-4

Work Therapy
#20166 $4.95   ISBN 0-87029-276-5

Everyday-courage Therapy
#20167 $4.95   ISBN 0-87029-274-9

Peace Therapy
#20176 $4.95   ISBN 0-87029-273-0

Friendship Therapy
#20174 $4.95   ISBN 0-87029-270-6

Christmas Therapy (color edition)
#20175 $5.95   ISBN 0-87029-268-4

Grief Therapy
#20178 $4.95   ISBN 0-87029-267-6

More Be-good-to-yourself Therapy
#20180 $3.95   ISBN 0-87029-262-5

Happy Birthday Therapy
#20181 $4.95   ISBN 0-87029-260-9

Forgiveness Therapy
#20184 $4.95   ISBN 0-87029-258-7

Keep-life-simple Therapy
#20185 $4.95   ISBN 0-87029-257-9

Be-good-to-your-body Therapy
#20188 $4.95   ISBN 0-87029-255-2

Celebrate-your-womanhood Therapy
#20189 $4.95   ISBN 0-87029-254-4

Acceptance Therapy (color edition)
#20182 $5.95   ISBN 0-87029-259-5

Acceptance Therapy
#20190 $4.95   ISBN 0-87029-245-5

Keeping-up-your-spirits Therapy
#20195 $4.95   ISBN 0-87029-242-0

Play Therapy
#20200 $4.95   ISBN 0-87029-233-1

Slow-down Therapy
#20203 $4.95   ISBN 0-87029-229-3

One-day-at-a-time Therapy
#20204 $4.95   ISBN 0-87029-228-5

Prayer Therapy
#20206 $4.95   ISBN 0-87029-225-0

Be-good-to-your-marriage Therapy
#20205 $4.95   ISBN 0-87029-224-2

Be-good-to-yourself Therapy (hardcover)
#20196 $10.95   ISBN 0-87029-243-9

Be-good-to-yourself Therapy
#20255 $4.95   ISBN 0-87029-209-9

Available at your favorite bookstore or directly from us at: One Caring Place, Abbey Press Publications, St. Meinrad, IN 47577. Or call 1-800-325-2511.